The

Color

of

Grace

The
Color
of
Grace.

*Thoughts from a Garden
in a Dry Land*

Tonia Triebwasser

Fleming H. Revell

A Division of Baker Book House Co
Grand Rapids, Michigan 49516

Published by Fleming H. Revell
a division of Baker Book House Company
P.O. Box 6287, Grand Rapids, MI 49516-6287

Printed in the United States of America

Library of Congress Cataloging-in-Publication Data

Triebwasser, Tonia, 1954–
    The color of grace : thoughts from a garden in a
dry land / Tonia Triebwasser.
      p.   cm.
    ISBN 0-8007-1775-9
    1. Gardeners—Religious life. 2. Gardens—Religious
aspects—Christianity. I. Title.

BV4596.G36 T75 2000
242—dc21   00-029097

For current information about all releases from Baker Book House,
visit our web site:
                 http://www.bakerbooks.com

Contents

5

JULY

AUGUST

SEPTEMBER

OCTOBER

November

December

Preface

Humanity's first glimpse of God happened in a garden. Since then we have tried to duplicate its beauty. We plant flowers, grasses, trees. Place fountains. Hang chimes. Augment anemic soils. We water, dig, and make our knuckles bleed. But Paradise eludes us.

Our gardens are environments of perpetual change. The cypress reach their heights of glory as the fruit trees wane. The daffodils finish their blooms just as the liquidambar begins to bud. Pansies and snapdragons wilt in the same heat that brings the roses alive. We are not dissuaded.

Just as a prism of glass miters light and casts a colored braid, a garden sings sweet incantations the human heart strains to hear. Hiding in every flower, in every leaf, in every twig and bough are reflections of the God who once walked with us in Eden.

❧ Consider the lilies of the field.
MATTHEW 6:28 KJV

A Lush Island
in a Swelling Suburban Sea

MY WORLD

As gardens go, mine is small and young, a lush island in a swelling suburban sea. No rambling meadows. No Bambi thickets. On three sides a redwood fence stands against an army of stucco houses. The fourth is bounded by an asphalt river flanked by a city sidewalk. Its crisp green lawn is edged with clumped perennial accents. Rosemary, mugho pine, fescue, and zephyr lilies, to name a few. Threads of pink gazanias, evening primrose, strawberries, and wild geranium stitch it all together. In the bare stretches of winter, chrysanthemums, autumn joy, bergenia, and stock bring promises of spring.

Along my garden's right arm runs a sidewalk edged in fern, lady's mantle, and baby's breath. Down its left shoulder is a stepping-stone path. Creeping thyme and ajuga winds between its irregular treads. In summer, a passel of old-fashioned hollyhock salute the clump of red-hot pokers opposite their post. Lobelia, sparaxis, roses, tiger lilies, coreopsis, and zinnias make revolving appearances.

I carve my solitude from a ceaseless urban drone. Neighbors to the south have toddlers and a beagle pup. Neighbors to the north have teenagers and parties with loud Spanish love songs. I borrow oatmeal from those to the south, aspirin from those to the north. I shave away the ringing phone, the rush of cars, yapping dogs, squabbling children. Just over the hill, bells from the cemetery ring. I carve carefully, deliberately, leaving its toll intact.

Over the years, I've learned to be content with my garden of hummingbird proportions. From Albania my aunt writes, "I have seeds and a planting pot, but the sun does not reach our balcony. I have no soil, and I am reticent to borrow even a shovelful from my neighbors."

My mother lives in the Sierra Nevada foothills. Her garden is immense, wild, well beyond her control. Last year she conquered the blackberry vines along the creek. This year they are back with a vengeance. "I haven't the strength to tear them out this year," she laments.

In my limited realm, I have endured conflicting seasons. I have been the mystic, claiming a false empowerment; the ascetic, inviting persecution; and an agnostic, shaking my fist in confusion. Exhausted, defeated, I fell silent, collapsed. I had mistaken labor for transformation. Dogma for faith. Illusion for reality.

In a brave moment, I viewed my diminishing reserves and admitted my intrinsic lack. I needed a Master Gardener. Someone other than me. Someone to water. Someone to usher in light.

❧

The roots of a small mesquite tree can travel as much as fifty feet to find water. My roots are weak. I am a Samaritan woman hoisting a bucket of false promises. Snails, butterflies, birds, snakes, frogs, and an occasional raccoon have made their way into my garden of faulty origin. A pristine, abandoned Eden returns to me transfigured on the scent of a rose. My garden mimes a paradise that is now off limits. I am barefoot with a leaking hose.

When my curiosity was larger than my wisdom, I crawled into a cave through a low, narrow tunnel. With one tiny flashlight, I made my way toward a pinprick of light. Past dark puddles, over damp muddy ground, I kept my eyes forward. At certain points, the tiny light seemed to widen, soar. Finally, the ceiling lifted. I got off my belly. In the center of the water-hewn cavern sat a stagnant pool pinging with condensation. No sweet aromas. No bright blooms. Nothing green. The light at the end of the tunnel was my own. A reflection off a dank pool.

Water and light. These are my garden's essentials. Even its shade has been chosen with care.

The trees closest to my windows are deciduous. In the fall, their leaves become a palette of red, yellow, and gold. In the winter, the sun shines through bared branches. The evergreen collects the sun and stores it up for winter afternoons. In the scent of its boughs I remember lengthened days and wind-freshened mornings.

Water and light. In the blaze of resurrection fervor, grace uncaps an impossible fountain. Surrender is my garden's cup. Prayer is its throat. Faith modulates the flow.

> ❧ *Now in the place where [Jesus] was crucified there was a garden.*
> JOHN 19:41 KJV

January

What We Hear in the Silence

NEED

January is a quiet month, a time of resolution. Eclipsed by the cold, the sun's vellum gaze does little more than sweep across the frozen ground. Birthed in its glance, ghosts of former seasons steeple forth and join the smoke of winter fires.

I study the sleeping bones of my garden. The camellias are fat with shade. Yarrow is dense, bristled like the coat of a wary cat. A blanket of mulch swaddles the geraniums.

Clanking along, pursuing the urgent, I leave big footprints in the noise. Footprints that prove I'm not a shirker. But now a brisk silence abounds. I am restless. Driven to make an impact, prepare an answer for the questioning pause. Every twig, leaf, and blade of grass is crusted in a rind of frost. But I am unmarked in the silence. Who am I in its growing hollow?

I can't stand it. I put on a sweatshirt and tackle the front flower bed. With a hand shovel, I have turned up the ground. The phone rings. I set my shovel down, misplace it. I make a hurried search. The shovel has vanished, is nowhere to be found. I picture where I think I left it. I fumble through the rosemary, sift through the bergenia. Empty snail shells. A gum wrapper. No shovel. Finally I ask.

"Has anyone seen my shovel?"

"It's on top of the red tool box."

Eureka. Right where I left it. If I had found it where I thought it was, what laws of nature would have been broken to make me correct?

❧

I knew a man who was mistaken for a caribou by a grizzly. He did the only sensible thing. He ran. Against everything, he ran. Fortunately, he stumbled. The fall saved him by interrupting his panic. Fighting against a powerful urge to curl up in a ball and pretend to be dead, he stood up and ran toward the grizzly. Shrieking and waving, he faced the superior presence. The bear stopped, cocked its head, turned tail, and loped away.

At root, I am a coward, a weakling. Hesitant to face what I cannot conquer. I want an ordered world. To be surrounded by that for which I can be proud. The lure of perfection is a homing instinct. A memory passed down to me from soul to beleaguered soul. I cannot abandon the search. Strangely enamored by this false possibility, I am driven to find what my forebears lost.

It cannot be. The gates to Eden are closed. Our own endeavor, sacrifice, or will cannot open them. We are sequestered to its outskirts for good purpose: We've poisoned the pot. Our very presence would track in mud.

Even in a world where there is no moral consensus, my heart knows the truth. I am of a conflicting blend. If I deny my goodness and say I am all bad, I am grotesque. If I deny my badness and say I am all good, I blaspheme. Denial is a subtracting process. In its constriction, I am apathetic, surreal, unapproachable. Honesty is my only solidarity, my redemption.

What does the silence say? I listen. Invite open dialogue. The God of my redemption has something to say.

> ✖ *Incline your ear, and come unto me:*
> *hear, and your soul shall live.*
> ISAIAH 55:3 KJV

Foxglove

Heart Medicine

The same heart-healing medicine found in the leaves of a foxglove can also cause a heart to fail. If love maketh a heart merry and also causes it to break, a medicine for its benefit would most certainly have similar risks.

Myth says a heart needs merely to receive love to thrive. But it is in giving and in receiving that the heart grows strong. Amateurs recklessly divvy it up. Exchanges are seldom equitable. Wounds are inflicted. Weaklings withdraw.

But love is a daring dance of surrender. A dance of courage. Love is a labored waltz. The speckled trumpets of the foxglove sound revelry to hearts waiting to dance.

February

A Season of Fearful Pruning

ANGRY CONNECTIONS

February marks a season of fearful pruning. Winter, which was only last month too rotund to get about, has now grown somewhat thin. Evanescent and anxious, it waits with packed bags for departure. New growth is on its way and seeks a vacancy. Armed with sharp, well-oiled shears, I anticipate the coming surge.

Trees present the greatest challenge to my skills. Branch structure determines a tree's stability. Like siblings, crowded branches vie. When massed, the wind can launch the entire tree on a tragic flight.

One can wax quite powerfully with a pair of sharp shears. I have learned to be careful. To begin tentatively. Thinking they should be treated like ordinary rose bushes, I pruned my climbers during their dormant season. Roses are tough. They survived. But they showed up in spring, limited and with their noses clearly out of shape. Two years ago in the heat of summer, I took the clippers to a flourishing butterfly bush. It never recovered.

A twig has to me an expression of purest happiness. It is not yet committed. Too fragile to be saddled with a rope swing, it sways alone, unhampered. No shade is demanded of its wave. It takes a scant toll on a flourishing tree and is a testament of the trunk's residing health. But as it grows, its relationship to the trunk becomes critical. I look for angry connections, a connection that takes a bud from twig to branch in a jackknifed position sending it through the middle of the tree rather than out toward the sun.

Unlike a new twig, life must upon its emergence be severed to survive. A baby's first cries protest its disconnection as well as announce its hunger, its need for warmth and comfort. The hand of time weaves larger bones, keener minds, and prompts a need to communicate. Our bodies change along with our needs. But the needs of the spirit remain the same. The needs of the spirit are those of connection. Above all, it requires union, to be known completely and still loved. Born to disabled arms, the best intentions of our parents fall short.

Connection is formed by anger. Anger makes an undiscerning cry. It tells us that something should be happening and is not. When we are angry it is because that which we expected has not occurred; that which we have prepared for is not forthcoming. Just as hunger cannot fill the stomach, anger cannot soothe us.

Connected to anger, the spirit dies. The sword of redemption renders the spirit viable. One side of the blade is repentance. It severs us from anger. The other side is forgiveness. It sears the wound.

Suddenly we are free to make safe connections. Unions with those who do not let us think we are more than we are. Unions with those who do not think themselves superior. We are free to connect with joy.

> ❧ *I am the true vine, and my Father*
> *is the gardener . . .*
> *apart from me you can do nothing.*
> JOHN 15:1, 5 NIV

Rose

A View above the Thorns

I once had a friend stroll through my garden. When she came to the roses, her eyes passed over the vibrant blooms and fastened on the thorns that lined their stems.

"I never could figure out why everyone makes such a big fuss about roses," she said. "All those thorns for a few pink blooms."

When God made the rose, he did not give it volition. Just life. It grows, blossoms, and exudes fragrance as a result of another's toil. God is not a thief. He will not invade that which he does not own. For that which is his, he provides and supplies. He wants to participate in our lives. To those who give him permission, he is an unfailing gardener.

God empowers the spirit to blossom along what may often seem a stairway of thorns. The path is steep. But the skies are watered with grace.

If by my wish my friend could see past the thorns to the rose, I would light a million candles and blow, blow, blow.

March

If It Acts Like a Weed,
It Is a Weed

FLAWED CHARACTER

March is a time of rampant nostalgia. As in the final days before Christmas, I am overcome with a hustle-bustle spirit. Remembering a host of former springs, I anticipate the one forthcoming to be the grandest of all.

Often enough, nostalgia skews my memory. I exclude unwanted details. Like weeds. And yet, along with the strawberries, the lupine, the daffodils, and the wild geraniums, the weeds march in. I run to get ahead of them. Wet weather puts up a roadblock. When the skies clear, the ground remains mushy, mired. By the time it dries, the weeds are thick and alluringly green.

Spring weeds are the queens of mimicry. I am not tricked by a name. If it acts like a weed, it is a weed. Weeds have no preference save that of neglect. Hard soil, scant water, insects—none of these deter them. Weeds take. They do not give. A flower returns the gifts of sunshine, rain, and labor with pleasing fragrance and color. Weeds yield nothing with consistency and order. If they ante up at all, it is with a fleeting bloom wrapped in scratchy arms. Weeds live in the voids. I hoe and mulch to keep them at bay.

Weeds are a sneaky lot. They grow among flower seedlings they most resemble. Spotted spurge intertwines with my isotoma. But come spring, there are no blue stars on its brow. It is found out. My evening primrose unwittingly hosts a weed with the same leaf structure and colors. Time soon tells the difference. When the primrose explodes with color, the weeds bring no gift to the party of blooms.

I made the mistake of planting a flat of violets. No mum was safe in their vicinity. They devoured my poppies, decimated my young delphiniums. It seemed wrong to pull them up. After all, they were quite charming in the spring. I wasn't sure it was worth the effort until after my poppies recovered and multiplied. My mums grew fat. My delphiniums made it through the winter. I've learned. I relegate mint and ivy to clay pots. I keep a close eye on the daisies.

It's not easy to keep a garden in a city of weeds. I live in an ecosystem aswirl with questionable seeds. They settle in quietly and invade forgotten fissures. Today I triumphed over self-indulgence, tomorrow I'm apt to wake up contentious, bent on gossip. Yesterday I was charitable to an obnoxious neighbor, tomorrow I might see her at the mailbox and pull the blinds.

Even the best of mulches, designed to keep moisture in and weeds out, can allow some astonishing guests. One summer I brought in a load of compost. I laid it down thick. In a place where I did not remember planting it, a robust stalk began to grow. Before long it developed a large prickly pod the size of a child's fist. I couldn't imagine what it was. I waited. After considerable time the pod burst open with a startling tuft of cotton. I kept the cotton and tore out the plant.

Whenever I design a perennial border, I am invariably asked, "Will it be maintenance free?"

"Maintenance free?" It's all I can do to keep from shrieking. "Cement is maintenance free."

Test the spirits to see whether they are from God.
1 JOHN 4:1 NIV

Canterbury Bell

An Unforgettable Song

For an entire season I waited, often wondering if I had not planted the Canterbury bells at all but tricky weeds. The stalks grew, stayed green despite the coldest nights. They put on height. The Dutch irises released their blue butterfly blooms. My snapdragons emerged and waned. My roses unfolded and blushed. Still, the Canterbury bells refrained from ringing.

Just before Easter a thickening began. Little green bumps appeared on the stalks. Green slowly thinned away to a soft purple tide. Rain fell for three solid days. The sun rolled over and slept. A piercing wind flailed the swaying stalks.

Unexpectedly, a white sun appeared, upstaging the mocking clouds. The storm fizzled and cleared. The Canterbury bells burst from the green stalks, tolling with purple peals.

Even still, my garden remembers their song.

April

Watching Spring

RESURRECTION LIVING

It is the first day of April. A green wind is singing. Through stalk, leaf, and petal receptors, my garden is hearing spring. The maestro is a glaze of protracting light. The grass ripples, bends. The liquidambar keens and soughs. Seed pods unclench, extend. In perfect time, poppies explode and twirl. A brown spider strums a silver web. Lamb's ears perk up. Candytuft and phlox intone with a scent of peach jam.

I sip coffee, listening, hearing a memory. I am huddled in the crook of a walnut tree's trunk. Midnight the cat is whipping her paws through the air, flicking the dirt with her tail. Flying, spinning, now rushing down. She is the Old Man;

the Sea is the dark hole at the base of my tree. Her paws dive deep. She has snared a fuzzy brown mole. I scold, plead. Tears roll down my cheek. The cat follows instinct and will not release its prey.

I cannot remember life without death. I do not gracefully bear its disruption and cannot learn to like it. All of life is lived within earshot of death. Spring is the song God orchestrated to comfort the grieving, the frightened, the celebrators of life. In spring's symphony, resurrection is reenacted, brought close, nearly conceivable. If spring does its job, it makes me stop dead in my tracks.

Jesus went to the cross willingly, suffering no illusion, no lapse of power, no miscalculation of plan. I believe his heart broke in the cataclysm of our rejection of his unwarranted love. We couldn't accept what we didn't understand, couldn't trust what we didn't earn. Our doubt did not change a thing. His death lit a resurrecting light. A fire of extraterrestrial proportions. Its spark grows in listening hearts. It is an infusing flame. Grace is the hand that tenders the wood. Faith strikes the match.

※

I am an urn of Adam's skin, the thickness of a lifetime. When kicked, I spill protesting blood. Each year, spring takes another swing at bringing me around. Spring sings a resurrection song I strain to hear. A woodpecker drums its red head against a cedar pole. Cumulus clouds rock in the promising wind. Gold sap pulsates in the boughs of the winter-charred oak. A robin chick sheds its itching egg. I press my ear to the earth.

Dry bones, dry bones, hear the word of the Lord.

※ *He who hears My word,*
and believes Him who sent Me, has eternal life . . .
and has passed out of death into life.
JOHN 5:24

Evening Primrose

Proving My Mother Right

When I brought them from my mother's garden, they were limp, weedlike. She called them evening primroses. She said they would multiply, be lovely in the spring. I was skeptical. I waited, watched.

By the end of March, their tall, spindly stalks grew hips. April wrapped the hips in pink skirts. Through the afternoons and into the moonlit evenings, the pink blossoms glow. Waiting at the base of each open blossom is another, still sleeping. It springs open the moment the current bloom wilts. The performance lasts for several weeks.

Each fall I give many away. I repeat my mother's assuring speech as cynical eyes scrutinize those gaunt, bare stalks. To those who guard and weed them through the fall and winter, these early spring performers wait, once more to prove my mother right.

May

Possessing the Land

Ownership

On a May afternoon, I stroll down the sidewalk, assessing my kingdom with a royal eye. On all fronts my bartered wealth is amassing. The yarrow transplanted from my mother's garden thickens like an exotic mane. My iris have doubled their ranks. My neighbor Mary's campanula has spread from sprinkles to puddles of blue. My sister's maidenhair fern flops onto the sidewalk.

When the sun goes down, it is still warm enough to stand bare-armed in the dark. I hear an owl question the dusk from a streetlight. Boxcars slam together in the switching yard and rumble in my spine. Mary approaches with her new grandbaby. The neighbor across the way returns a mower, screeching like a giant pinned hawk, into a crowded shed. On the air the scent of barbecued hotdogs mixes with the green juice of cut grass. This is the community in which I live. Its members are the cultivating tools the Creator has used to reveal the wilderness within me.

I am selfish. I do not like to share my planet. I want to be first in line, to sit in the best seat, to get the best buys. I do not willingly make room for others in my schedule. And I am hard-pressed to recognize my self-serving ploys. In a meadow of lupine, with a full belly and a calendar empty of appointments, I convince myself of sainthood. It is community that finds me out. My family, constituents, neighbors—these are the tillers of my soul.

When we moved here, our lot was waist high in weeds. I knew no one. We lived on a dead-end street. To the west and northwest were open fields, dotted with oak and vernal pools. I ruled a priceless view. When the sun set, I watched it fold into a drawer of pink dusk. Now when the sun is still high, overlapping roofs of multiplying houses snuff out its dramatic retreat. The road attaches to a main artery. The biggest mall in northern California is being built within walking distance.

I am searching for the bottom rung on the ladder of a great shrinking hill. The valley is fat with houses. Remaining bare land is scarce, expensive. That which remains lies in lean, sparse strips. Mine is a city of mavericks, entrepreneurs who work alone and congregate on the Internet. Modern technology has engendered extreme efficiency. But the fallout is an accumulating loneliness, the symptoms of which are all around us. Having been told they are the children of the earth, our youth grieve an aging mother and bury prayer sticks in her stratified folds. Does a man cry sap, or a woman give birth to a twig? We are not the earth's children. The earth is our collective gift, a birthright we have squandered for meals of convenience and greed.

Ancient prophets went to the wilderness to discover what we ignore. God speaks through the land. It is a testament of his glory. Proof of his omnipotence. But it is art at which to marvel, not to worship. Their stints in the wilderness were short-lived, a time set aside so they might become familiar with the voice of their Creator. From there they were sent back to dwell among the cultivators of the soul, back to the regions where the words of the Creator could be tested and they could be living examples of the Creator's continuing intervention with the family of humankind.

※

In a small fenced yard, the sun warms the forehead of a child teasing a stray cat with a red ribbon. On a signaled boulevard, modern warriors ride wide arrows with ball-bearing wheels. They conquer the curbs, the concrete steps, and squawk like taloned birds. Between narrow canyons of concrete and steel, someone smokes a cigarette and lets the smoke relieve his tears. Where is this land of milk and honey? Someone needs to tell them. They have a right to know.

We have a divine parentage, a Creator who is not improved or impaired by our awareness of his art. The promised land is not a geographical location, not a plot of pristine wilderness to be staked off and claimed. The promised land is a refuge, a territory of reborn spirit.

> *I am the door; if anyone enters through Me, he shall be saved, and shall go in and out and find pasture.*
> JOHN 10:9

Delphinium

Well-Structured Support

Delphiniums, those glorious jewels in a garden's crown, are not easily won. When small they can be devoured in a single evening by a snail the size of a thumbnail. If they live past infancy, they require considerable water. They must be fertilized and protected from weeds. Once mature they boast such robust blossoms, staking is required.

The supports of a delphinium are nothing of which to be ashamed. In fact, the grander the bloom, the more necessary becomes a well-structured support. The density of her blues makes the delphinium unable to stand alone. The weight of such a hue can send her crestfallen into the mud. The very process of lifting a fallen bloom can cause her to snap.

A delphinium will grow improperly supported. Its color will be vivid, its scent sweet, its nectar rich. But its petals will be stained with mud.

June

What Is Time to a Gardener?

Growth

Sashaying in on white-hot legs, June starts the race of summer's growth. French lavender, daisies, gaillardia, roses, and coreopsis spring from the gates. Chamomile sprouts yellow wings. Lemon thyme explodes in a curling purple mist.

A bumblebee escapes in the folds of a rose. A skirmish breaks out by the finch house. Three finches twitter, tisk, vanish. The tiny house remains vacant. A praying mantis snatches a butterfly from midair. Orange wings flail against a sword of strapping legs.

At last, a soft breeze releases a river of cool air. The shadow of the birch stretches in the sun.

From towering boughs, shifting green shade serves saucers of relief.

I water. Steam rises from the patio, reviving a scene of kick-the-can and blindman's bluff. Oh, to be like the bumblebee and escape in a rose. Yet, just the right size to cruise downstream in a leaf. Thumbelina. Stuart Little. Tom Thumb. These little folks knew how to redeem the time.

Time is a gardener's best friend, a horse to be ridden. But time is change. With any luck, time does away with the small. Generally speaking, it takes seven to ten years to develop a garden's upper story. A magnolia won't be rushed. Rhododendrons are unaffected by applause. A clematis sets its own pace to scale a wall. Vertical plantings, vines, and trees raise the ceiling of my garden, taking the eye up. The finest gardens rise as lush as they reach. Reds blend with blues, yellow drips on white, green steps up the back of greens. As growth takes on height, new space opens up below. The shade shifts. Sun-loving plants must be relocated. Shade-lovers, hydrangeas, ferns, azaleas, take root where hollyhock once thrived.

Invariably, a garden reaches back. Its present structure is closely linked to the past. I set out to define my garden, but mysteriously, it defines me. I chose its structure deliberately. The grapevine that hugs the arbor was not planted for its fruit. I wet the leaves and see the face of my old school chum, Karen. Her hair is curly, the color of snow. Her cheeks are red, her forehead sweaty. We are seven and out of breath. We have outsmarted the enemy. The boys next door have lost our trail. Karen's grandmother's vineyard has drawn its arms around us. We peek out, giggling, watching the boys' bewilderment with growing satisfaction. Children live for the thrill of the pursuit.

My liquidambar gives me another view. I see my mother lifting them out of one-gallon cans, placing them in freshly dug holes, her hair held back in a thick ponytail. Last month I drove by the old house. Those liquidambar are now thirty feet tall. I wonder when mine will catch up with hers?

❧

At dusk the nightingale finds its way to its podium on the crook of my weeping cherry. Its song rings out repeatedly. Stuart Little returns.

I join him in his leaf boat and ride its melody up a flight of the sixteen wooden steps that lead to my childhood bedroom. Beneath the memory of a black-and-white checkered bedspread, I recall past spring mornings and the familiar song from the throat of my nightingale's distant relative.

Five years ago, my weeping cherry sprung a blister in its trunk. I was told to rip it out. Instead, I painted it with white paint, trimmed off the dead twigs. Give it time, I say, give it time. It makes a strong perch for the nightingale.

> ❧ *Neither he who plants*
> *nor he who waters is anything,*
> *but only God, who makes things grow.*
> 1 CORINTHIANS 3:7 NIV

DAISY

High Tea

Daisy, daisy, give me your answer true. . . .

Believe me, they will. Daisies gush. The daisy's outbursts are a wonder. An exclamation. I keep an eye out, monitor their numbers carefully. Flowers on their perimeters could be easily squelched.

Were they members of a choir, the director would forever warn, "Pipe down." Were they guests at a potluck, the daisy would be first to go for seconds. But I can always count on daisies to round out a mixed bouquet. A handful of daisies and a rose, a lilac and a lily can turn a table of tuna sandwiches into a high tea.

July

Things Unfamiliar

CHANGE

By midmorning, the sun is a hot kettle. I feel it through the walls. It has sent a blast of steam through the shingles and into the attic. I scurry about the yard, looking. Somewhere there is a hidden pot, boiling dry on a forgotten red burner.

A heat storm. That's what the experts called it last night. Nineteen days (today makes it twenty) over one hundred degrees. I am stuck in a season of heat. A universe of technology and still no one can find the burner and remove the pot.

I hide from the heat as I hid last January from the wind and the cold. The air conditioner runs equal time with last winter's heater. Both extremes smack of a conspiracy. I hose down the garden, hopping from shade patch to shade patch.

Tuberose does well in the heat. Its scent, delicate and far-reaching, bubbles up from a stiff wand of waxy white, clustered petals. I tolerate the heat long enough to breathe in a chestful of its scent.

With the sunset comes the buzz of crickets sounding like errant amperage crackling in a cave. "The coast is clear," they buzz. "Come out, come out, wherever you are."

How can I resist? I bend close to the base of a climbing rose, digging in with my finger to see if any moisture remains in its hot bed. Nose-to-nose with a black and yellow racer, I spring back. The snake is calm. It stays fixed, wrapped like a ringlet around the thorny base.

The snake is said to be good for a garden, but I am not pleased by its presence. It has a suspicious persona. No arms, yet it can hang onto an ankle as well as a rose. Its skin looks wet and slippery, but it is dry and rough. No legs, but it moves swiftly.

I escape the valley's heat by visiting a friend on the coast. An old friend. When I arrive, she brings out a thick pile of letters. Letters we've exchanged through the years. I begin to read, and groan. Much of what concerned me then, concerns me now. I had wished for more progress. I'm beginning to understand my childhood nightmares of going to school naked. They were not Freudian fears at all. They were warnings. Premonitions. This is what it is like to grow up. You have to be willing to show your self. Your whole self.

I once held a notion that a garden reaches a point of self-containment. I could not have been further from the truth. A mature garden needs constant intervention. Whatever I neglect finds me out. Points a finger. But my strength, as well as my time, is limited. The afternoon sun sits in a position that, if I point, draws my arm into a Nazi salute. I refuse. The sun has tyrannized me enough today. I could deadhead the zinnias. Clip back the spirea. I leave it all for another day, go inside, and thumb through the old letters.

After two hours, I am still reading, appalled at my own stagnation. The sun has dropped below the crown of the oak across the street. My front yard is immersed in its shade. I love that old oak. It stands on a lot destined for development, surrounded by a protective fence. "Come this far and go no further," the fence seems to say. "Do not disturb." What I need is a disturbance. Something to jar me from complacency.

Unlike the oak, I need examination to grow. My letters thrust my feet to the flames. They show me where I have remained compacted, desolate, unfruitful. I am stubborn, frightened. I have a strong will. A thick skull. I need help. Divine intervention.

I must not emulate Eve, who at her greatest moment of need hid from God.

> ❧ *Examine me, O LORD, and try me;*
> *Test my mind and my heart.*
> PSALM 26:2

Coreopsis

The Color of Grace

I love my coreopsis. These little chips of sun sparkle through May and June and into July. They need little in the way of maintenance, water, or fertilizer. I can neglect them. The snails can't hurt them. The weeds can't choke them. The coreopsis is an incorrigible bloomer through the hottest summer days.

"What color is grace?" I ask God.

"The color of coreopsis," he replies.

"But that doesn't make sense," I exclaim.

"I know," he says with a silent, affirming nod.

August

August Is a Blabbermouth

SACRIFICE

A garden party in August is a risky affair. August is a telling month, a blabbermouth. The most critical guests will be those who have never laid a glove on a shovel. Not knowing a lick about how to keep the worms off the petunias or mildew off the zinnias, armchair gardeners are slow to appreciate what seems to weakly abound. They scowl at what used to be snake heaven and jackrabbit Shangri-la, looking for fuchsia and orchids. Where are the koi ponds to soak their swollen toes?

But I'm not one to talk. I have been known to jump to similar conclusions. It serves me well when I stop and gather the facts. Walk a mile in their shoes. This is the spirit I need to adopt. Shoes can look terrific while causing excruciating pain. I, at all costs, want to avoid pain. Yet pain is both the sickness and the cure.

In the spring, every gardener is young, uncalloused, and full of blind ambition. Spring gardeners are the looky-loos. The misinformed. When the pony packs dry up unplanted and the peppermint chokes out the peony, they retreat, pour a glass of lemonade, and thumb through seed catalogs, dreaming of fairy-tale flowers and mythical fruit.

Reality is. Period. I am only one woman. One shovel. One hoe. As much as I would like to think otherwise, it took me overly long to recognize what I could change and what I could not. It wasn't for lack of advice. And it wasn't just recognizing my limitations. It was separating fact from fiction and allowing for the value of mystery.

The yarrow at the base of the liquidambar needs more sun. My climbing roses sprawl in the wrong direction. Feverfew doesn't sit well with climbing hydrangea. These are things I can change. I would much rather meander through the aisles of a shaded nursery. Choose a flat of poppies and envision them in the ground. I know better than that.

It is the August gardener who stumbles out at dawn. Dusk finds her wobbling in with blistered hands clutching a fragrant bouquet. An authentic gardener is constitutionally incapable of leaving a pony pack to dry up overnight. She could no more yank the top off a weed and leave its root intact than paint the white camellias red.

> ❧ *Whatever your hand finds to do, . . .*
> *do it with all your might.*
> ECCLESIASTES 9:10

Snapdragon

A Remedy for Lethargy

We all know about the snapdragon. Hers is a blossom that doesn't tolerate extremes, be it heat or cold. Keep an eye on her mouth. For it is the mouth of a snapdragon that reveals her overall condition. If, when pressed gently on either side, it does not curve skyward, she is suffering from heat exhaustion. If the top petals protrude beyond the bottom petals, check to see if worms are hiding within the folds.

I have an overall healing remedy for the fragile snapdragon. Take a moment to indulge her. Recount for her all the sudden bouquets she has inspired. Sift out the clod at her roots. Remove the stones. Finally, feed her a cup of cooled alfalfa tea.

September

A Penchant for Rocks

FOUNDATIONS

In the rapidly diminishing fields flanking my neighborhood are nests of moss-covered rocks. Plans for more homes and a mall are on the horizon. I make inquiries, call the owners. Would it be all right if I removed the rocks before the bulldozers arrived? Yes. They give me permission to have as much as I can carry. In the softening glare of the September sun, I scour the surrounding fields. Pick and shovel in hand, I fill the back of a borrowed pickup. And another.

And another.

I come from a long line of rock collectors, a peculiar mixture of masons and preachers. At the nape of my garden's neck runs a miniature wall of river rock nudged into place by my father's patient trowel. The home of my childhood was warmed by three of his stone fireplaces. My mother's garden was laced with stone retaining walls, including a moon gate designed by my father with river rock. He learned his art from my grandfather, who, in between sermons, built fireplaces and stone walls in a manner passed down to him from his father. And so it is natural that I would carry on this family tradition.

After much heaving and straining, I find enough rocks to form a low wall. Instead of the mortar my father would use, I join the rocks with patches of campanula, prunella, lamb's ears, and various sedums.

Standing back, hands on hips, I recall another hunt that uncovered an altogether different treasure. In the basement of our home, I had rummaged through a box of odds and ends, looking for who knows what. I ran across a box of what I thought were Chase Colonial chocolates. Though I would have been satisfied with the lesser gift of candy, I opened it to find an assortment of rings set with polished gems. Thinking I discovered a box of sudden wealth, I ran excitedly to my mother. In a manner that has since been repeated, what was new to me was old hat to her.

"The rings were your grandfather's," she said. He used them for props. Reading from Revelation, he would list the various gems in the foundations of heaven. Jasper. Sapphire. Chalcedony. Emerald. Sardonyx. Sardius. Chrysolite. Beryl. Topaz. Chrysoprase. Jacinth. And amethyst. As he came to each stone, he would hold up the rings.

Judging from the frequency of their use in Scripture, God is, apparently, fond of rocks. Rocks make good foundations. They hold things together. Scripture recounts rocks as being used for altars, for protection, for dwelling places, and as markers of God's goodness. Many miracles are connected with them. At God's command, water, as well as fire, sprang from rocks. The wise are described as those who build upon rock. A certain kind of rock. Five of which David used to slay Goliath.

I have giants of my own to conquer. Unlike the Philistine brute, my Goliath resides within me. A giant of fear that lurks upon every unfolding horizon. My stones are these: truth, faith, perseverance, discipline, and love. In the heavy rains, these little stones keep the soil in my garden from rushing away. In drought, the rocks keep the moisture in. During winter, the rocks store the sun and warm the soil beneath them.

Except for its rock moorings, my garden changes before my eyes. Intermittent crisp evenings edge the leaves of the liquidambar in pensive color. Only last week they were predominantly green. Today they are edged in yellow, some in red. Tomorrow they will be altogether crimson. In increments they will fall to the ground, exit on the wind. The thinning catalpa leaves are being transformed daily with a deepening wash of lemon-pie yellow. Engorged with scarlet juice, the fruit of the pomegranate tree wrestles its branches to the ground. One by one they fall. In spring the cycle begins and repeats. The rocks remain.

We live on a planet that is slipping away. But the New Jerusalem will have a twelve-layer foundation. A foundation of refined stones. Stones refined by the Alpha and the Omega.

Imagine. This is permanence of which we are alien. A permanence for which the human spirit was designed.

> ❧ *Upon this rock I will build . . .*
> MATTHEW 16:18

CALLA LILY

A Rainbow through the White

I believe God intended the calla lily to wear a gown of many colors. But she did not trust his handiwork. Before he could complete her raiment, she fled from him. Wearing only one uncolored swath, she stayed in the farthest regions of Eden. Peering from the shade, she tried to gather enough evidence to prove he was worthy of her trust.

"He won't know what to do with me," sighed the lonely calla. "I'm not like all the rest."

The Creator, in his sovereignty, extended grace to the calla. He honored her choice to withdraw from his perfecting process. He gave her sunshine, water, and just the right amount of fertilizer, hoping she would see his goodness and submit to the completion of the task he had begun with her. God is still waiting.

In the shadowy corners of my garden, I have planted calla lilies. Their white fragility brings to mind a patient Creator. On moonlit summer nights, when the heat still lingers in the air, the calla seems especially visible, and if my faith is particularly strong, I see a rainbow through the white.

October

Dreaming a Garden

Plans

In October the sun grows weary and meek.
Plants become drowsy, threatening to nod off.
Like children, plants are most easily rearranged
while sleeping, which makes autumn a perfect
time for transplanting. A few high-strung daisies
have trampled the lawn. Renegade coreopsis
have ransacked the coral bells. I grab a shovel.
Divide. Reassign.

Myself, I've never been overjoyed about moving. For twenty-seven years my husband and I
have lived within a thirty-five-mile radius, but
we moved often during our first years of marriage. The thought of moving was always sweet-
ened by the possibility of finding the perfect

home. Alas, the perfect life. Transforming a house into a home, a yard into a garden—these were clearly defined, attainable goals.

When I was pregnant with our first daughter, we bought some acreage in the foothills. We had a tremendous view of the Sacramento Valley and the Marysville buttes. Our little brown mobile home was small, drafty, slightly sloping. It didn't matter. It was temporary. Our dream was underway.

We spent hours thumbing through magazines, choosing floor plans, walking the parameters of our property, picking the best place to plant our dreams. We moved bare-root fruit trees into the ground. Bought calves to raise for beef. Made houses for ducks and hens. We pumped water from the pond and diligently moved the heavy irrigation pipe from one end of our property to the other. The cows grew. The irises bloomed. We felt the baby kick. And then winter set in. Things changed. One day the heifers jumped the fence. Raccoons raided the chicken coop. I miscarried.

A dream takes its first breath from the heart. When the heart breaks, an awakening takes place. A sudden and questioning awareness which overwhelms the startled dreamer. Our hope was shattered. Our hearts were broken. For a succession of seasons, we could not hazard hope.

The disappointment of loss is unique to everyone. We weren't sure what we felt. Or for how long we would be feeling it. Weren't all things supposed to be working together for good to them that loved God?

Didn't we love God?

Our loss upset our measure of truth. When what we hoped in proved false, we began to doubt other things. Recovery was slow. Even today, after raising two wonderful daughters, we remember the loss of our first.

To move a rose requires as much strength as vision. Although they are particularly adaptive to a variety of soil conditions and exposures, roses do best in full sun and well-aerated soil. Two summers ago, I moved a rose for the second season in a row. It had only just begun to do well in its new location when I decided it was blocking my view of the grape arbor and, upon reflection, I realized it was in a spot best suited for a pond.

The rose is now doing much better than it had in its original position. And it doesn't block my view. I have learned to be a flexible dreamer. It will be a long time before my garden is as I dream it to be. I am constantly rearranging, revising. The coneflowers that were once in the front yard are better suited to the back next to the ruby glow. The butterfly bush rotted and had to be replaced with Mexican sage.

At last the rain appears and gives me a worthy excuse to head indoors. I put on the coffee. Light a fire. I sip and muse. Will I be around to see my camphor tree soar over the neighbor's shed? When will the creeping fig hide the splitting fence?

For Thou art my hope;
O Lord GOD, Thou art my confidence
from my youth.
PSALM 71:5

Coneflower

The Tallest Flower in the Garden

Among the tallest flowers in my garden is the coneflower (echinacea). I plant coneflowers in the back of my borders. Its blooms begin in midsummer and continue until the first frost. I love to watch the development of a coneflower's bloom. First I see a green pointed ring that looks much like a miniature crown. As the petals form and turn pink, the centers puff and glow orange at the tips. When the coneflower reaches full bloom, its petals curl under, its center mounds to a glowing ball. After the petals drop off, I dry the centers and save them for wreaths.

I planted the coneflower because of its appearance. Afterward someone told me echinacea tea is good for flu and colds. I thought maybe I could just shred the petals in a pot of boiling water. But, "No," I was told. "Healing comes from its roots, roots free of contaminates."

November

Why the Hummingbird Hums

PRAYER

Today there are storm warnings. Through the window, I watch the wind's blustery, unpredictable dance. Embraced against its will, the branches of the ancient oak rise and fall, groaning from limb to limb. Seeking a more willing partner, the wind swoops down and twirls the hummingbird into a reel. In a burst of resolve, the tiny bird breaks free and hums for cover in the spirea.

I know why the hummingbird hums. It is not because she doesn't know the words. She knows thousands of words. Splendid words. Eloquent words. There is a sacred language through which the soul does speak. Who has earned the right to hear?

Take Jack. Jack-in-the-pulpit. Jack uses the entire winter preparing his sermon for spring. Just above his winter bed, a praying mantis cocoon mutely clings to the fence, waiting. In mid to late spring a two-foot tendril rises, curtsies, and Jack's sermon begins.

I had a grandfather who was a little like the hummingbird and a great deal like Jack. Grandpa was a respected preacher. When his five children were small, his young wife, my grandmother, died of pneumonia. He was left to raise the children alone. As was the custom of the times, and understandably so, he sought a mother for his children and quickly remarried. Under the circumstances of grief and need, the union was fragile. In the years that followed, Grandpa was pulled in three directions—to his children, his marriage, and his ministry. Relentlessly, he begged God to rectify the troubling marriage. And though the relationship remained strained and volatile, he continued to preach the Word of God.

He spent countless hours on his knees discussing the situation, asking for protection for his children, understanding of his wife, and a blessing on his ministry. I believe it was my grandfather's prayers which gave his posterity a heightened spiritual awareness.

Thus far, his children have borne him twenty-four great-grandchildren. Each of us carry the story of Grandfather's mysterious faith. We are a family of music and drama and art. We sing and paint and plant, each of us articulating our faith in mediums that speak in ways that words cannot convey.

My grandfather died with many of his prayers unanswered. I would like to have asked him questions about my relationships and fluctuating faith. We could have compared notes. In times of unanswerable mystery, I remember the life and witness of my grandfather and I act cautiously. I understand how my choices will impact the generations that follow. I want to stay faithful to the God of my grandfather's salvation. My grandfather could pray for me, but he couldn't choose for me. He couldn't leave me all the answers, but he did teach me who to ask.

I am my children's history. I leave a map in the shape of an arrow pointing away from man's wisdom. Tell God. Ask God. These were my instructions. These are my instructions. God knows the language of our souls. In the seasons of storm, in the seasons of thanksgiving, bring your tales to the God of ongoing translation.

But the Spirit Himself intercedes for us with groanings too deep for words.
ROMANS 8:26

GARDENIA

The Scent of Heaven

I have often looked to no avail for the flask of perfume
beneath the white-glove petals of the gardenia. Its scent,
like the gentle hands of a patient mime, transcribes a
sense of place I cannot quite pinpoint. A place of soft
light and pillowing earth? Or is it an island of caressing
tides and clear seas? A high perch above the smog but
below the snow line?

As a mother's hand lifts her child's face in the
direction of a star, the scent of the gardenia is the
fragrance of things to come. A carrot before us.

I predict the gardens of heaven to be ruffled with
gardenias. Palm-sized blossoms exuding the same rich
scent save one startling difference: The heavenly
gardenias will be impossible to bruise.

December

Noel Sunshine

SYNTHETIC LIGHT

December marks the season of diminishing light. Light I try to duplicate in my garden. Leaves of the coral bells glow crimson. Burnished strawberry plants peek from the rug hooked with Mother Birch's fallen gold. English daisies, like little candles, sputter along the edge of the sidewalk. These, like the tiny Christmas bulbs I trim my windows in, are synthesized lights. Lights of comfort. Warmth. Bravado.

There is something mysteriously attractive and alarming about light. The very thing in me that craves light can also raise Cain against it. Light, a complicated subject. As much as I claim to need it, to seek it, to instinctively gravitate toward it, I've been sideswiped a time or two. Walked into the light unprepared for the view.

Yesterday passed beneath a pewter sky of fog and undelivered rain. The valley was a cauldron of gray mist. Somewhere above, the sun supposedly shone. I stood high, walked tall and couldn't find it.

Temperatures were predicted to drop last night. Frost warnings went out. I bundled up and hosed down the garden.

This morning, spun with fingers of moonlight, the lace of frost glitters and blinks from the still edges of leaf and blade. The garden is a cathedral of ice buttresses and frost steeples. It is remarkable to me how a sprinkling of water protects a plant from freezing. It works like this. The water on the outside freezes. Insulates. Acts as armor against the killing cold. The moisture on the inside of the plants is protected. The frost that gardeners fear, and rightly so, is not the frost that collects on the outside at all. It is the ice that develops on the inside. Ice that halts the cycle of growth and prevents sunlight from continuing the very photosynthesis that makes life viable.

Which brings me back to light. Light, and the frostlike fear that shields me from it. When I have been "illuminated" in an area I have inadvertently ignored, I am cautious about sharing. Sharing a new discovery about something or someone else is something I do naturally. But the new things I find in me—these I am careful about. Words erect markers around the discovery. I would prefer the light to fall on something good I said or did. But if it is on a thought I should have been able to control or a deed I wish I hadn't done, I feel shame, confusion. If I am to move beyond it, I must bring it further into the light. Confess it. If my listener gives me a raised brow, I wonder, Is my assessment credible? Is it earned? Did I make this all up? I rethink things. Ask more questions, letting my words bring yet more light to the dim territory.

My idea for a stepping-stone path was met with groans. Especially when I said I wanted to use chunks of cement from a refuse heap. I couldn't properly describe my idea; I had to show it. After the steps were arranged, ground cover bedded down between the treads and flanked with various perennials, I got a different response.

"Oh, is *that* what you meant?" It was fear that asked for approval, fear that doubted, and fear that almost discouraged me. Had I given in, the path between the fence and my garage would still be a soggy strip of flourishing weeds.

God knows about show-and-tell. And yet his greatest performances are preceded with an echoing prologue. Fear not.

Fear not, Abraham.

Fear not, Joshua.

Fear not, Zacharias, Joseph, Mary.

Fear not, shepherds.

God understands my fear because he put it there. The very fear that prompts me to run from God's brilliant proclamations is tethered by his spellbinding creations.

Is it any wonder God chose to meet humankind in such a puzzling form? Doesn't everyone love the sight of a newborn baby? I will run to soothe a baby's cry. But when the baby grows into an omnipotent Savior, I want to stop my ears. Why? What makes me now afraid to hear?

Last night while I slept, the rain lambasted my pansies. This morning they lay prostrate in the mud. I gently washed off the bark and sand from their petals. Flicked off the heavy drops of water. Pinched off the spent blooms. They stood up and teetered bravely in the breeze. Would he who calls himself the Master Gardener do anything less for me?

❧ Christ has brought you into the very presence of God, and you are standing there before him with nothing left against you—nothing left that he could even chide you for; the only condition is that you fully believe the Truth, standing in it steadfast and firm, strong in the Lord, convinced of the Good News that Jesus died for you.
COLOSSIANS 1:22–23 TLB

A Word of Caution

Too much gardening is risky. Stripped down and closely examined, gardening is merely a rewarding hobby. For all its noble appearance and aesthetic contributions, it is a luxury. There is no denying its rewards. But it is easy to become obsessed. I know.

A flower is neither good nor evil. It is beautiful. Fragrant. A tree gives shade not to benefit another, but because it cannot choose not to. I must choose. Each day, choices must be made. I am a wife, a mother, a daughter, a friend. In these roles, I am planting seeds. Seeds which I may or may not see develop, but seeds nonetheless. This kind of planting takes prayer. Constant and fervent prayer.

May the bulk of my kneeling take place not before a garden's fleeting beauty but before my Creator's hidden and holy throne.

> ❧ *Let us therefore come boldly unto the throne of grace, that we may obtain mercy, and find grace to help in time of need.*
> HEBREWS 4:16 KJV

Tonia Triebwasser is a poet and writer of both fiction and nonfiction. She lives in Sacramento, California, with her family and her suburban garden.